INSIDE THE AUDITION ROOM

The Essential Actor's Handbook For Los Angeles

INSIDE THE AUDITION ROOM

The Essential Actor's Handbook For Los Angeles

By Jason Buyer

ISBN 978-0-557-93943-5

Preface

The odds of making it as a working film or television actor are slim. Just look at the statistics.

Approximately 250,000 actors in Los Angeles are pursuing careers in film and television. Of those, 118,000 are already members of the Screen Actors Guild, or SAG. Over 80 percent of all SAG members won't even qualify for health benefits, unable to earn the $9,000 yearly minimum required for eligibility. And only 2 percent of all actors in the union are considered to work at their profession full-time, earning more than $100,000 per year.

In my 12 years of casting films and television shows, I observed hundreds if not thousands of actors, even ones with exceptional talent, making critical mistakes in and out of the audition room that hurt their careers. Most of the time, actors aren't even aware that they are sabotaging themselves. And very few professional organizations offer in-depth courses on what to expect when you arrive in Los Angeles—or what to do after you get here.

Don't get me wrong. Talent is extremely important. But it is simply not enough. In fact, based on what I've witnessed in the audition room, I believe talent can only account for about 50 percent of your career success. For the other 50 percent of your livelihood as an actor, you might as well get yourself a business degree—or, better (and easier) yet, read this book.

Inside The Audition Room: *The Essential Actor's Handbook For Los Angeles* has been designed to provide you with the fundamental career-building knowledge of the industry, teaching you how to combine the business of marketing with your talent as an actor. This book breaks down exactly what casting directors are looking for, and comes to you straight from inside the audition room. We welcome you inside.

Acknowledgements

I am proud to say that many of my closest friends are casting directors, agents, managers, photographers, and current and former students. It has been nearly ten years since I began teaching the formula to my students, and I am eternally grateful for everything I have learned in the process. There are so many people to thank, but this book would not have been possible without the love and support of my family, especially my wife Melissa and two daughters, Lily and Josie. I want to express my appreciation to my mentor, Jeff Ginsberg, and my Columbia College family in Chicago and Los Angeles, who have opened their doors and given me a platform to grow. This book, however, is dedicated to the thousands of actors I have had the privilege of working with over the years. I have become a better person and teacher because of you.

Contents

CHAPTER 1

WHAT YOU MUST KNOW

This Is A Job Interview – Arrive On Time

Prior to any audition, most actors will usually spend 10 to 15 minutes performing various vocal exercises or mouth stretches, warming up their vocal instruments. After all, if a casting director can't hear or understand you, what's the point of coming in to audition?

What most actors aren't aware of, however, is that it also takes the casting director, producers, and director several minutes to settle in and warm up. That's right: They, too, need time to adjust to their new surroundings and prepare for the next task, reading talent and casting the project.

In other words, it takes time for everyone on both sides of the audition room to focus.

So, why would anyone walk in to audition when the casting director, producers, and director aren't yet ready?

The answer is obvious. You wouldn't. Or at least you shouldn't.

That's why I always tell actors to stay clear of being the first actor in the audition room, just in case the casting director isn't quite mentally prepared for what's ahead. That isn't to say that the first person in the room never gets cast. But why not increase your odds?

Most of the time, casting directors will bring in actors based on when they arrive or sign in. Depending on the size of the role, theatrical (that is, film and television) casting directors will see an average of 4 or 5 actors every 15 minutes. If you have a 9:30 a.m. audition time, expect to see other actors reading for the same project, and sometimes the same role, at the same time.

So give yourself a cushion. Let your competition sign in first. After all, it's always nice to have an opening act before the main event hits the stage. If you can, try and avoid being the last person in the audition room as well. That's not to say that the last person in the room can't be cast. But at the end of the day, or near lunchtime, casting directors and other industry professionals get hungry and often tired, or bored, just like real people! Of course, you might just get stuck with the last audition time that is available that day. Don't worry, go in and do what you have been trained to do. Look on the bright side: It's better than no audition time at all.

Be on time for every audition. In fact, treat your auditions as if you were going in for a job interview. You may arrive at least 15 minutes prior to your appointment time, but not any earlier. Most industry professionals prefer you not to wait and mill around their office space. And you should never expect casting directors, producers, and directors to wait for you. If you are running late, don't expect them to wait around, even though they don't mind if you wait for them.

I remember when I was working on the Annie Potts series, Any Day Now on Lifetime, also starring actress Loraine Touissant (Friday Night Lights). The series was already in production, doing well in its time slot. I was the casting associate, and was in charge of setting up all of the casting sessions for the series. I had scheduled actor Rafael Sbarge to come in and read for the producers of the show for a recurring role. You may remember Rafael Sbarge playing the role of Glenn from the movie Risky Business. Scheduling actors for Any Day Now was always a challenge, because all of the casting sessions were located in Santa Clarita, CA. Not convenient for many actors, especially with LA traffic. As we were approaching the end of this particular casting session, I noticed that Rafael was a no-show. His representation confirmed him, and had guaranteed me that he would be there. Unfortunately, our producers needed to leave and couldn't wait for Rafael any longer. As we were driving away, I saw Rafael run into the production office. He left a few seconds later, defeated, and visibly upset because he missed his audition. The moral of the story: Don't be late, because CD's won't wait!

Remember: You have one shot at every audition. Make the most of it. It's best not to miss it because you happen to be stuck in traffic or running late. The reason you are late won't matter to anyone but yourself.

Lost Isn't Just A TV Show

Getting lost is no longer a viable excuse, but it's still the one I hear most often when I'm casting a project. Why would any casting director, producer, or director expect an actor who can't find their way to an audition to show up on time for an actual job? Better yet, to follow any type of direction - even in front of the camera?

Great resources exist today which can help you find your way. The internet offers terrific websites, including MapQuest and Google Maps that will enable you to print out or download directions straight to your audition destination, whether you're traveling by car or public transportation. Many cars now come with built-in navigation systems; or you can buy a GPS system for your car. Many cell phone applications can get you there, too. And of course there's the old-fashioned way: buying a map or asking friends or family for directions.

In Los Angeles, most locals have or know about the Thomas Guide, a bulky map book, sold in bookstores and drugstores everywhere in Los Angeles, that puts the entire vast metropolis on a grid system and offers an alphabetical index of every street in the city. It's always a good idea to have a Thomas Guide handy, and those Angelinos who know it keep it in the glove compartments or trunks of their cars. You never know when you're going to get the call for that last-minute audition, and you can be sure a Thomas Guide will help you get to your next audition on time.

Agents & CD's – Your Teammates

Inside information gives any actor an edge. That's why I recommend that you get your hands on an agency and casting director guide.

You'll find many different types of guides available for purchase. I emphasize such guides because casting directors themselves use them. The information they offer is essential to promoting your brand. You'll find a more detailed explanation of how to use them in a later chapter.

Breakdown Services offers a seasonal Agency Guide and Casting Director Guide, available at www.breakdownservices.com. Or you can purchase them at any outlet of the Samuel French Bookstore, which specializes in books related to film, TV, and theater. Again, it's the information that's important, and overall a relatively inexpensive hit to your pocketbook.

How and When to Become a Member of SAG

If you are an actor pursuing a career in film and television, you will eventually want to become a member of the Screen Actors Guild, or SAG. There are currently five ways an actor can become eligible for union membership. *(For eligibility in your state, contact your local SAG office, or check out www.sag.org for more information.)*

1.   **Get three SAG vouchers doing "extra work."** When you arrive on set to do extra work for the day, it is essential that you ask for a SAG, or union voucher. Ordinarily, unless you are already in SAG and have signed up to do union extra work, you will sign in as a non-union performer, and receive a non-union voucher. Ask for a union voucher. When you've collected three union vouchers, you will have become eligible to join SAG. (Note: If you are a minor, the union vouchers are only valid if they come through consecutive work days. If you are over 18 years of age, the days you work as an extra do not have to be consecutive work days.)

2. **Book a speaking role on a union project.** Any non-union actor who books a speaking role on a union project is eligible to join SAG. *(Also known as SAG eligible or SAG – E)* Once eligible, you will be able to audition for both union and non-union projects. However, once you pay your initiation fee and join SAG, you are no longer allowed to audition for non-union work. I suggest that you stay eligible for as long as you possibly can. Once you book your second union job, you will have no choice but to join the union and pay your initiation fee (known in the industry as a "must join"). If you have already received three SAG vouchers doing extra work, keep them until you are ready to join. There's no rush. You may even want to call the SAG office just to make sure your information is in the system, in case SAG decides to change the rules of eligibility. As a general rule, however, stay eligible as long as you can.

There was a time when I, too, had the acting bug and wanted to pursue my dream in front of the camera. I was just coming off an exhausting stint as a casting assistant, and realized that I missed many aspects of performing. Getting my degree in theater never allowed me to learn what was needed to pursue a career in film and television. I didn't realize the vast differences in audition styles until I was hired as a casting assistant, seeing firsthand what the casting director, director, and producers were looking for in the audition room. Although most of my acting experience was on stage, I felt confident that being in the room and running casting sessions gave me a leg up on my competition. My one issue, however, was that I was a non-union actor. I was determined not to let my non-union status hold me back. I reached out to my casting contacts to let them know of my new plans, and they couldn't have been more supportive. In fact, this particular casting office helped me get my SAG card. I was hired as an extra on the set of Pamela Anderson's syndicated show, VIP. I was going to be upgraded on the set, thanks to the casting director and producers of the show. As I sat with all of the other extra's on shoot day, I knew that I was going to be pulled aside and given a line of dialogue – an upgrade on set, that had been pre-planned. A real line of dialogue! Four and a half years of college for this one moment! I felt I was ready, and that I somehow deserved it. I can recall being admired by all of the other extra's on set, because I now had a line of dialogue, with star Pamela Anderson.

I became SAG eligible when I received a speaking role on a union project. To this day, I still receive the occasional residual check.

3. **Become a member via AFTRA.** I would not recommend this approach unless you have a connection to an AFTRA show, or have additional funds available at your disposal. Anyone can join AFTRA, (American Federation of Television and Radio Artists) which is the sister union to SAG. If you're an AFTRA member and book a principle (speaking) role on an AFTRA show, wait one year - you would then be eligible to join SAG.

4. **Book a national commercial.** This is probably the best and most lucrative way for any actor to become eligible for SAG membership. Commercial agents do not require actors they represent to be in SAG in order to take them on as clients. Most theatrical agents do, however. Commercial agents will submit you for both union and non-union commercials, regardless of your union affiliation. Booking a commercial seen nationally is the best way for any actor to become SAG-eligible. There is nothing like auditioning for a commercial and knowing that you are the choice – not to mention the compensation you will end up making.

5. **Be "Taft Hartleyed" by a casting director.** A non-union actor will always find it easier to sign with a commercial agent than with a theatrical agent. The main reason is simple: It is much harder for theatrical agents and managers to get auditions for the non-union actors they represent. Most theatrical casting directors do not

want to read non-union talent over the age of 18. But the Taft-Hartley Act, a federal law passed in 1947 and named for the Senator (Taft) and Congressman (Hartley) who sponsored it, sets certain controls on how labor disputes should be settled. Applied to working actors, Taft-Hartley makes it okay for a non-union actor to take a union job over the thousands of union actors casting directors have to choose from. Although some casting directors still Taft-Hartley actors, it is extremely rare, but possible. Some have equated the process to winning the lottery. The casting director fills out a Taft-Hartley form with all of the actor's pertinent information, (headshot and resume attached) along with why the actor should be hired. SAG takes a special look at why a casting director is trying to Taft-Hartley an actor. Special circumstances that have been approved by SAG in the past include matching the physical features of other actors who have already been cast as family members; the actor is a child, under 18 years old; the actor can breathe fire, etc. (Rare skills called for in a script or role can often get an actor eligible for union membership).

Production companies can expect stiff fines if SAG doesn't approve the reason for hire, which falls squarely on the casting department.

CHAPTER 2

HOW TO SELL YOUR PRODUCT

You Are Officially Open For Business

Want to optimize your chances of being cast? Then start thinking of yourself as a business, rather than as an "actor." Just like any business, if you aren't making money, your business fails. You are the product, and you need to make sure that your product sells.

The next time you are at the grocery store, take a glance at the toothpaste aisle. Look at how many different types, kinds, flavors, sizes, and overall varieties of toothpaste there are on the market. Why do you choose one over all the others? That's the same question casting directors are asking themselves everyday when setting up casting sessions. Depending on the project, casting directors have thousands of actors to choose from. Why should they choose you? In other words: Make sure you're a product worth buying!

The Casting Process Begins: Breakdown Services

The first thing that happens in the casting process, if things are running smoothly and on time, is that the casting director will receive a script. After reading it, the casting director sends the script to Breakdown Services, a company that breaks down the script by character. Some casting directors prefer to have Breakdown Services write the breakdown, while other casting directors prefer to write the breakdown themselves, for individual roles or entire projects. Casting directors will then begin to create lists for each role.

The first list will contain a list of celebrity clientele, who are "offer only" types of performers. The term, "offer only" refers to a small group of actors who have reached a certain level or status within the industry and no longer have to audition; they just receive offers. It is then up to those actors to accept or reject the roles they are offered. It is worth noting that a celebrity or name may be attached to a certain project prior to the start of casting. There are two advantages to this process. First, it gives filmmakers the opportunity to get funding or increase a pre-existing small budget. Secondly, having a name attached to your project can attract interest from studios and networks, as well as other high-profile actors whose name recognition can increase the odds the project will be made, bought, or put on the air.

While waiting to hear if the "offer only" actor or actors have accepted their offer, casting continues. The second casting list consists of actors who would go straight to the producer session. Pre-reading or pre-screening is not necessary. The casting director already knows their work, and is confident they will be great in the audition room. Most importantly, these actors will still come in and read for the producers, and make the casting director look good in the process.

And then there's everyone else: actors who have been submitted by their agent, submitted by their manager, or who have submitted themselves - all in hopes of getting the opportunity to read and be considered for the role. Once the breakdown is released, thousands of online thumbnails will be submitted, as well as hundreds of 8-by-10 hard copy submissions, actor drop-offs, as well as countless phone pitches. Depending on the project, of course, you are talking about a pool of hundreds of thousands of actors that are submitted on a daily basis for any given show or role.

When Is The Casting Concept Meeting?

While the casting office is being inundated with submissions, the next step in the casting process is scheduling the casting concept meeting. The casting department sets up the casting concept meeting to discuss all of the characters in the script. The producers, unit production manager, writers, line producer, casting director and director will all be in attendance. ("Offer only" casting lists are also passed out and discussed at this meeting, in case the producers prefer to make offers after the concept meeting.) By the end of the casting concept meeting, the casting department will come away with three very specific characteristics for each character in the script: the character's age, ethnicity, and a prototype for the role, such as a James Dean type.

After the meeting, the casting department will make any necessary changes to the casting lists, update and check on the status of the breakdown (based on the ideas and goals from the casting concept meeting), and make any offers, if the producers and director have agreed to do so. I have enclosed an example of a casting timeline for episodic television below.

STEP 1
CD gets the script from the producers.
CD begins making lists. Offer list, producer list, and pre-read list.
Breakdown Services breaks down the script by character, or the CD writes their own breakdown.
Casting concept meeting is scheduled.

STEP 2
Casting concept meeting is held.
Possible offer to be made.
Breakdown of all of the characters is discussed, including the age, ethnicity, and prototype. Info is then added to the breakdown.

STEP 3
Breakdown is revised with new information and then released to all agents/managers.
CD's begin to go through all online submissions.
Hard copy submissions arrive and are sorted.
Pre-read casting sessions are set up and scheduled.
Producer sessions are scheduled.

STEP 4
Pre-reads begin.
Producer sessions are confirmed.
Casting checks in to see if the offer has been accepted, if made.

STEP 5
First producer session.
Roles cast, if choices have been made.
CD receives day out of days (shooting schedule)

STEP 6
Second producer casting session scheduled (if needed)
CD begins to close deals and book actors

STEP 7
Table Read

Most of the actors I went to school with are no longer in the business, so I am grateful that I am able to do what I love. I consider myself one of the lucky ones. I remember my first job in casting and my first casting concept meeting, working as the assistant under Mary Jo Slater, who is Christian Slater's mother. At the time I was hired, I didn't know anything about casting. I started as an intern, and got called in to Mary Jo's office with a potential job offer. I remember Mary Jo asking me what the minimum amount of money I would need to make in order to "survive", as she put it. I found this to be an odd question, but wanting the job, I knew that I would have to throw out a low number in order to beat out my competition. I said, "I could do the job for $400.00/week." She said, "How about $350.00?" Without blinking an eye, I said, "You got a deal." Boy, did she ever! What a negotiator!

I had a lot of flexibility as the casting assistant at Slater and Associates Casting. I wasn't sure if it was because it was so incredibly busy, or if Mary Jo believed that I had a knack for finding new talent. One of the last projects I worked on in that office was for the syndicated show, Soldier of Fortune, where I had the opportunity to read and set up a casting session for a five line co-starring role. One of the actresses I brought in was Selma Blair, who was undoubtedly the best actor I read that day. I certainly don't think that I discovered her, but I do feel proud that I helped her book one of her very first jobs in the business. She was, and still is a true talent.

Once the casting director receives the official breakdown, a final edit will be made to it, including the characters' age range, ethnicity, and prototype, if available. As soon as the breakdown has been approved by the director and producers, the casting department will release the breakdown to all of the agents and managers. Agents and managers will then have the opportunity to go through their list of clients and submit the clients they feel fit the character description, submitting online or via messenger, with the clients' 8-by-10 picture and resume. The casting department will specify on the breakdown if they prefer electronic or hard copy submissions. Sometimes the casting director will ask for both; but 90 percent of the time, a casting director will only ask for you to submit online.

How Casting Differs from Project to Project

While the general description above applies to just about any project for which you might audition, there are certain things you will need to do to the text based on the specific kind of project that is being cast. A basic understanding of how to break down your text will help you approach any casting call with more confidence, and give you the clarity you need in the overall process.

Unfortunately, there are too many qualified actors that may be "right" for the role. The job of the casting director is to simply cast the show. Knowing the genre for which you are auditioning will help you make strong choices to the material, and greatly improve your chances of getting called back.

Half-hour Comedies

A half-hour comedy is on a five-day shooting schedule. This means that the casting department will receive a script on Monday, and by Friday the episode will be close to completion. A casting director will schedule one casting session, with the possibility of a second session, if casting is having difficulty or in need of holding callbacks. Because time is so limited for casting each episode, the casting director sometimes won't even hold a pre-read session.

Within the category of half-hour comedies, there are two basic kinds: the traditional "sitcom," short of "situation comedy"; and the more contemporary single-camera half-hour comedy. It's smart to go into a casting call knowing the basic differences between them.

Half-Hour Sitcom	Half-Hour Comedy, Single-Camera
Script is written in double-spaced format.	Script is written in single-spaced format.
Shot on a soundstage, in front of a live audience.	Shot on location, without an audience.
Multi-camera: a three or four camera show.	Single-camera.
Laugh track.	No laugh track.
Examples: Friends; How I Met Your Mother, Rules of Engagement	Examples: The Office, Parks and Recreation, 30 Rock, Modern Family.

The Drama/Dramedy

A one-hour drama and one-hour dramedy (a term referring to a drama with comedic elements) that is currently on air will have a shooting schedule of eight days. Casting will try and schedule two casting sessions, since they will have more time to audition before shooting begins.

Drama

Text is single spaced

One hour in length

Lower energy

Not funny

Audience has to catch up to the action in the scene

Example: CSI, House, The Good Wife, The Mentalist

Dramedy

Text is single spaced

This genre is a combination of:
- ½ hour sitcom
- ½ hour comedy; single camera
- 1 hour drama

One hour in length

Audience has to catch up to the joke or action in the scene

Example: Glee, Castle, Desperate Housewives

Pilot

A pilot is the first episode of any new show. Although it is on an 11-day shooting schedule, casting will have several months to find the leads or series regulars before the pilot begins shooting. If an actor books a pilot, he or she will be paid a one-time pilot fee, plus a separate per-episode fee if the pilot gets picked up—that is, bought by the network.

Feature Film

Although you may audition for feature films, it's possible that an offer has already gone out, or in some cases, been accepted for the role you are auditioning for. A film always has a better chance of surviving if a name is attached to a project. Remember, casting directors will always schedule a casting session just in case the offer doesn't go through. (This is also true for all episodic television casting.) A casting director will usually have a month or two to cast the remaining leads and supporting players in the film. Film casting has always been list-heavy – names, names, and more names. As mentioned before, most film actors won't come in and read, having already proven themselves in the marketplace. If a casting director is interested in a name actor, they will have to make a straight offer.

One of my favorite casting stories comes from the time I was working at Slater and Associates Casting. I was working with casting director Bruce Newberg on the feature film, "One Legged Cricket." I was fortunate enough to be in the room and run camera during all of the casting sessions. Because this was a major feature film, we were able to attract big name actors to come in and read. I remember Jennifer Love Hewitt, Elizabeth Berkley, Brittany Murphy, and Famke Jansen all coming into the office to pick up scripts. The first casting session for "One Legged Cricket" included Freddie Prinze Jr, and actor Jeremy Sisto. You may remember Jeremy Sisto from the feature film, "Clueless" and "White Squall." I was running the camera in the audition room, along with CD Bruce Newberg and the director, who had an unopened bag of red Twizzlers licorice with him. When Jeremy was brought in to read, he greeted us and made a bee line towards the licorice, opening the bag. To our amazement, Jeremy began eating the licorice as he began his scene. I have never seen anything like it - he was fearless. The scene certainly didn't require him to eat, but he did and in the process, took complete control of the audition room. We realized very quickly that we were no longer auditioning him – he was auditioning us! Jeremy ended up being the top choice for the role. Although the film ended up losing its funding, it still makes for one of my favorite audition stories to date.

Project Headshot: The Never Ending Project

From my experience working in some of the biggest casting companies in Los Angeles, and quite possibly the world, I have found that the more specific you are with what you are selling—that is, what differentiates you as a particular kind of actor—the better chance you have of getting into the audition room. In other words, stop selling "actor" and get specific with your headshots.

Remember, your headshot is your calling card. It is sometimes the first introduction many actors have to the casting director. It can't just be good – it needs to be great. Your competition as an actor is huge – well over 250,000 in Los Angeles alone, with half of the actors in LA already members of the Screen Actors Guild. The simple truth is that I don't want you to be or to think like most actors – too many of whom aren't working!

The trick is to minimize your market so you can maximize your marketability. If I put out a breakdown for a teenager, I will receive thousands of headshots that look like teenagers, most of them looking similar and very generic. If I put out a breakdown for a male teenager, 15 to 18 years old with a punk rock look, that market is cut in half. If I put out a breakdown for a male teenager, 15 to 18 years old with a punk rock look, who knows how to ride a unicycle, we're talking about a small handful of actors. Your talent will matter once you get in the audition room, but you have to get in first. I recommend trying to sell three different versions of you, while using your environment to help sell your product. Stop selling the general, non-specific "actor" headshot. Become a type.

Pick A John. Goodman or Stamos?

Most actors reading this will probably assume they can play both character and leading roles in film and television. After all, it's only natural to want to do both. However, the worst thing you can do in this industry is to blend. It's hard to get noticed when you blend in, because no one can see you! If you aren't selling something specific based on the characteristics of the breakdown, you won't fit into any pile except the trash.

It's time to get specific and decide how you are going to sell yourself. Are you going to be a character actor or a leading actor? Pick one. You'll have the option of playing many different types of roles later in your career, when casting directors become familiar with your work. If you decide you are a leading man, your direct competition will be in the Jared Leto/Zac Efron market. Attention all six-pack owners: This is probably your market! If you are a leading female, you will end up going head to head in the Kristin Stewart/Sandra Bullock market.

There are two main characteristics for all leading actors, which can be broken down into physical and intellectual characteristics.

For example, James Denton is a leading actor based on how he looks physically. James Spader is a leading actor based on his ability of playing intelligent, intellectual roles. Both of these actors are leading male types, although look very different.

Character actors have the option of selling different types of characters within several different headshots, such as the lawyer shot, teacher, mother, bad guy, villain, dad, victim, drug addict, popular kid, nerd, and so on.

There is also the combination of the two, the leading character type. John Goodman is a leading character type—a character actor who plays leading roles. The more he works, the easier it is for him to transition into either market. It's still believable that he can play the dad, lawyer, villain, and bad guy.

In brief, always know what you are selling, and what your market is. If you don't, you certainly can't expect your agent or manager to know. Most importantly, being a character actor may not seem as glamorous as starring as the lead, but character actors work!

Character Exercise:

Make a list of at least ten different occupations or types you feel you can play best, and then narrow it down to the top three roles that you feel you can play today. If you can only come up with five or six choices, that's okay; but be creative and experiment with your list. Ask family, friends – even people that you don't know. They all may be able to help you get specific with what you're selling.

Turn on the television and see who and what types of roles are currently being cast – and who is already dominating your market! We always see ourselves differently than other people do, so ask around. Sell your type based on how you currently look and present yourself. If you don't look homeless, you probably shouldn't sell homeless as a type. There will be plenty of actors that actually look (and may be) homeless that the casting director will bring in for the role. It probably won't be you.

It's extremely important that your headshots look like you when you walk in the audition room. We don't want you to be acting in your headshot, because we won't believe you! Try to sell three different versions of you, using your environment to help sell your product. Don't forget to make sure that the background is blended and out of focus. You never want to steal focus away from your product, and what your product is selling.

Include a personality shot as one of your three specific headshots. The personality shot can be used as your commercial headshot; it should show you smiling, with great energy. Commercially, you may want to use a headshot that is more general, in hopes of becoming the spokesperson for lots of different products or companies. Commercial casting directors are always looking for real people, with a great personality, smiling, and plenty of confidence. For film and television, however, you will want to sell two or three different versions of you. You will be called in based on how casting directors perceive you, and your type.

Don't Judge Me!

As an actor, you are constantly being judged, critiqued, and picked apart. Get used to it. Casting directors will go through a stack of headshots like a deck of playing cards. It is your job to make sure that your headshot stands out. Is your headshot going to make casting directors stop shuffling the cards?

With so many headshots submitted online today, it's not easy to get a computer thumbnail (your headshot on a much smaller scale) to stand out; finding one that does can be extremely difficult, even more daunting than picking out your favorite look. Your best headshot will always be the one that is selling something specific—that is, strongly portraying a particular kind of character or type, rather than the one that makes you look the prettiest or most handsome.

How much time do you think it takes a casting director to decide whether or not to call you in? Not long: maybe a minute, or even a few seconds. It's so important to make a positive first impression – this is your business! Don't settle on having just a good headshot, when great marketing materials are within your grasp. You are only helping yourself and your business (not to mention your agent or manager) in the long run, so get specific and make sure your headshot pops off the page.

It's Okay To Typecast Yourself

I usually get in a lot of trouble when I tell actors they should be typecasting themselves, but I feel it's necessary based on status of the industry today. Los Angeles is inundated with actors all looking for work. Most actors will tell you that they are right for the role, and could play the part. The problem is there simply aren't enough parts. Most casting directors, producers, agents, managers, and directors don't know about you and your business – yet.

When you have a career like that of Tom Hanks, with scripts piling up on your front door, feel free to play as many characters as you want. You will have the clout to do so. Until then, get specific with what you are selling, and remember that your best selling point is YOU.

Consider: Why does Madonna have such a fabulous career? She is always reinventing herself and constantly selling something different. She knew when something wasn't working, and was brave enough to change her product when she needed to. Whether you decide to be a character or lead, try to typecast yourself two or three different times. Sell two or three different versions of you, and see what CD's end up buying.

Looks Like You Could Use A Career Makeover

Plan to use your specific headshots for at least two years. Once casting directors are familiar with your work, you may make the transition back to a more general headshot.

Now, I know actors, and most of them are antsy, wanting immediate results. If this is the case, review your materials after a year and a half and tally up how many auditions you have had, and list the types of roles you have been called in for. For example, if you are selling lawyer, villain, and popular guy, and notice that you have never been called in for the villain, chances are casting directors may not perceive you as being able to play that type. Go back to your list of occupations and types, and try selling a new product, while still using the headshots that have worked for you in the past. Your progress should be based on what you continue to audition for and, hopefully, what you continue to book.

If you feel you are not auditioning enough, based on the three products you have chosen to sell, you may want to consider a career makeover. Put simply: Doing whatever it takes to sell your product - losing weight, gaining weight, cutting your hair, dying your hair, changing markets (going from lead to character, or character to lead), and so on. In other words, change! For example, you may never work as a blonde with long hair. It's possible. Instead, most of the work you book may be as a brunette with short hair. Although you have to give casting directors enough time to get familiar with what you are selling, be open to the idea of selling something that industry professionals respond to or perhaps want.

What I Like About You

Go to the movies or turn on the television, and you'll see that you don't have to be a great actor to work. You simply have to sell something that people want. Keanu Reeves (sorry, Keanu) is a perfect example. He's pretty much the same in every movie, but that's okay because he's selling something that people want; he knows his audience as well as his own strengths. He may not be the greatest actor, but he is a very smart actor with a business that is thriving.

Every actor has a niche, whether it's comedy, drama, a funny laugh, or being the bad guy. It's your job to find your niche and sell it! The roles you have been auditioning for in the past are key to discovering what your niche may be. How do casting directors currently perceive you? Can a casting director easily recognize what you are selling in your headshot? What headshots are casting directors responding to most? Sell something that people want and watch your business thrive. Once you know what your niche is, try selling it until you are ready to sell something else. By that time, you will have enough clout to make the important decisions in your career.

CHAPTER 3

PROMOTING YOUR BUSINESS

How are you promoting your business? The good news is that there are many different ways to self-promote you and your business in addition to the specific headshots discussed in the previous chapter. Remember: No one will care more about your business than you do. If I asked you how you would sell yourself, would you know what to say? Promoting your business is going to be a very important part of becoming a working actor. If you haven't promoted yourself before, don't worry – just start now.

You've Got Mail

Regularly sending out 4-by-6 postcards of your headshot (or headshots) is a great way to stay in touch with industry professionals, including casting directors, producers, directors, and any other industry-related contacts you may have made over the years. When I was casting, I loved getting mail. It always seemed that an actor would send a postcard at just the right time, usually when I was in a pinch and having trouble setting up my casting session. Postcards certainly aren't as bothersome as phone calls, so it was always a nice break to receive mail from an actor, sometimes an actor I had never met.

The overall goal of self-promotion is to be remembered, which is what a postcard can do. Remember, the job of a casting director is to simply cast the project. Casting directors don't have a lot of time, between setting up sessions, closing deals, taking verbal pitches over the phone, making lists, setting up the table read, and on and on and on. Time is a casting director's number-one nemesis! If a casting director had more time, they could do so much more, like read more actors! Postcards allow the actor to keep in touch, at an arm's length, which is what most casting directors prefer.

Note: An actor may put two or three different looks, or products, on one 4-by-6 postcard. However, your 8-by-10 headshot should only sell one occupation or type at a time.

As you are creating your business plan, try sending out postcards every six weeks. Use your agency and casting director guides to make a new industry contact. It's a great way for you to introduce yourself. Get in the habit of sending out postcards on a somewhat consistent basis, without getting overwhelmed with what to write on the back of them. Here are some ideas you may use on the back of the postcard, just to break the ice:

"I just arrived from _____."
"I just reshot my headshots with _____."
"I'm currently looking for new _____ representation."
"I'm currently studying with _____."
"I just went to producers for _____."

If you happen to be sending a postcard to a casting director, don't be afraid to compliment them on something they've recently cast, like a new TV show that got picked up or a film that has just been released. We all love when our hard work is appreciated.

Business Cards

Having a business card with a small version of your headshot on the front is another way of self-promoting your business without being too bothersome. It's just another device to help industry professionals remember who you are, which is why you are promoting yourself in the first place. Do what you need to do to be remembered. When you are meeting someone for the very first time, hand him or her a business card. If you introduce yourself and tell me you are an actor, chances are

I'll forget. Give me your business card with your headshot on it, and I'll have a way of remembering you.

Drop-offs

Many casting directors, especially commercial casting directors, share office space. A drop-off is when an actor stops by the office to drop off a headshot for an agent, manager, casting director, producer, director, etc. The process is quite simple. An actor takes his or her headshot and places it in the mail bin, or hands it to an assistant, based on a particular project or as a general submission for representation. Your headshot may now be looked at and considered. Drop-offs are not always the answer and don't always work, but I certainly wouldn't tell an actor not to do them.

Cold Reading Workshops

Cold reading workshops are another great way to get in front of a casting assistant, casting associate, casting director, agent, or manager. A cold reading workshop can be a one-time class, or several weeks with the same instructor. The goal is to be called in to audition. Be careful, some cold reading workshops have a better reputation than others. I have included some general guidelines for you to follow if you decide to do a cold reading workshop.

1. **Be a great cold reader.** If you are not a great (notice that I didn't say good) cold reader, you should not be cold reading. Actors are usually paired up with another actor, and have about 10 minutes to review the sides before performing. That doesn't give you a lot of time to prepare and make strong choices with the material. Chances are it won't go well unless you have mastered cold reading and its technique. Why show anyone in the entertainment industry a mediocre product? You wouldn't, so don't. Learn the skill first.

2. **Do your research.** There are several cold reading workshop companies in Los Angeles. I used to be an invited guest at numerous workshop companies and I have always found that the companies who audition actors always produce better talent.

3. **Surround yourself with the best.** As far as talent goes, it is so important to work with an actor that can hold their own in a cold-reading situation, and make you look good. Remember why you are doing these cold reading workshops in the first place. If you are a good actor amongst a group of lousy actors, the casting director still won't call you in. If you are a standout amidst a group of great actors, a casting director will feel much more confident about bringing you in to audition.

4. **Don't expect too much.** Look at a cold reading workshop as an opportunity to be seen, not as an acting class. Workshops can be great practice when you are ready, but usually very little instruction or feedback takes place. All of the instructors receive an honorarium to be there. Sure, they would love to discover someone, but is that hidden gem really going to be taking a cold reading workshop? Probably not. When I was casting, I probably called in a total of 35 actors to audition for various roles, over a period of 12 years. I had my own private workshop folder, and when the opportunity arose, I would reach into that folder and call someone in - just not very often. For the record, however, two actors I read years ago at a casting director workshop are now on a series, and one of them is an Emmy nominee. You just never know!

Celebrity Scramble

As I mentioned earlier, if you don't know how to sell yourself, you can't expect your agent or manager to be able to do it. The truth of the matter is, they just won't know how to do it. This is why it's so important for you to know your type.

The celebrity scramble is the combination of two different celebrities that you have been compared to, combining looks and personality. People say that I am a cross between Adam Sandler and Ben Stiller. Is it true? Who cares! Again, it's all about being remembered, and everyone knows who they are. It also brands me and my type, which is so important to do as an actor. After all, there aren't too many people in the world that will have difficulty remembering Adam Sandler or Ben Stiller. This is a social tool, and if used correctly, can define your type and create your niche. It's effective, especially if you don't know how to sell yourself.

Making Friends Outside Of Facebook

Who you know will play a very important part in your career. Was there ever a time when you were at a social gathering and saw someone you wanted to meet? How many times did you go the extra mile to introduce yourself? The truth is, you just never know what doors will open if you just put yourself out there and take a chance.

Imagine the people that are already in your life. What did you do to open those doors? Was it worth the risk? Are you glad you took the chance? Say a producer you worked with five years ago signs on to do a television pilot that gets picked up by CBS, and there happens to be a recurring role that you would be perfect for. Will you get the opportunity to audition? Will you be remembered? Maintaining those relationships will always give you a greater chance of getting what you want.

You should keep an ongoing list of everyone you have ever met in the entertainment industry. If you don't have a master list, start one now. Your list should include names, company names, job titles, addresses, phone numbers, and email addresses, as well a brief description of your relationship. (This new list will become a part of your mailing list when you send out postcards.)

Keeping a list of your industry contacts doesn't mean that I want you to ask anyone for a job or audition. The goal is to build your relationships, so when a casting director is looking for your type, they will remember to call you in first.

IMDB On Paper

The trade papers will also play a part in your career. *The Hollywood Reporter* and *Variety* are basically the same type of trade paper, giving you the latest information on movies in production, casting, and box office sales. If you ever want to know who is doing what, pick up one of these trade papers (you don't need both, so save your money) or register at IMDBpro.com. It's important to know who's running the industry that you want to be a part of. Remember, you don't need to be a working actor in order to know who's working. It's a worthwhile investment.

Backstage West (or *Backstage East*, depending on which coast you are on) is a trade paper I would recommend for those of you who are new to the industry. It has plenty of casting notices, so you will be able to submit yourself for potential acting jobs, including student films, independent films, and theater. I also recommend *The Hollywood Creative Directory* and *Ross Reports*, both publications filled with invaluable information for the actor.

The Players Directory

The Players Directory is a valuable marketing tool which actors should be familiar. In order to be in *The Players Directory*, you must be a union actor or signed with an agency that is in the union. The directory consists of several volumes of pictures, or headshots, all categorized by type. Once the casting director starts to receive submissions, casting will begin to look at all of the thumbnails, and start setting up their casting sessions. The director, producers, and writers may add or delete characters within a script at any time. This is where *The Players Directory* comes in. Upon finishing the script, casting directors will use The Players Director for casting ideas, especially when the CD is in a pinch. The directory has become an extremely useful tool for actors, too. A couple of things you will want to know about The Players Directory:

- You must be a union actor or signed with a union talent agency in order to be eligible for *The Players Directory*. No exceptions.

- There is a fee of $30.00 per look ($60.00 per year), or sign up for a recurring payment and pay $18.00 per look ($36.00 per year). There is also a free online listing at www.theplayersdirectory.com. You can choose from several categories: Adult Male, Adult Female, Young Adult Male, Young Adult Female, Character/Comedian, and Kids. Pick one. Because you are only selecting one look or type, post your favorite, more general headshot when the time is right.

- Even if you are in a union, I would wait until you have legitimate theatrical representation (do not post your commercial representation) before registering for *The Players Directory*. Remember: management or agency representation only.

- The Players Directory is located at 2210 West Olive Ave. Burbank, CA 91506. (310) 247-3058.

Getting Ready For Your Close-Up

Now, don't get me wrong, you don't have to be out every night of the week promoting your career as an actor. But no one is going to know about your product if you stay home every Friday night. Getting people to remember you is a full-time job. So get to work!

Plays are always a good idea—at least during the months of April, May, and June. The busiest time you will have as an actor is during pilot season, which comes after the first of the year and runs through the end of April. Feel free to ask your agent or manager, but I can tell you that it's probably not a wise idea to get cast in the touring production of *Fiddler on the Roof* in February. You'll have a hard time getting anyone in the industry to come and see you in a play, especially during the busy season. You also won't be able to audition for anything else, since you are already attached to another project. It's okay to audition for plays; just plan ahead and be smart about it.

Participating in a showcase is another great way for an actor to be seen. A showcase is a group of actors who perform two-to-three minute scenes in front of industry professionals. A showcase can take place over the course of several nights, or on a weekend. Actors will pay a one-time fee to participate. Again, this is another opportunity for actors to be seen by those that matter most—agents, managers, casting directors, directors, and producers. Impress them, and it will be money well spent.

The "You" Network

A demo reel is a two-to-three minute commercial selling you - using film, television, and commercial footage from jobs you have previously booked. Your demo reel shouldn't be any longer than four minutes, and should feature your best material first. (Most casting directors won't watch the entire thing). Any clips of you with a celebrity should also be included.

Having a reel or footage of your work can only make it easier for your agent or manager to pitch and sell you to a casting director. Know that the content and quality of what's on your reel does matter. What are some of your projects shot on? Digital video or 35mm? It makes a difference.

Most importantly, if you don't have great footage of yourself as an actor, don't put together a reel. It's better if you wait until you have something worth showing. If your performance isn't strong, or the quality of the production is grainy, why show it to anyone? Just because you have it doesn't necessarily mean you need to use it.

Work on putting together a great demo reel, and then pay for someone to edit it professionally. Agents and managers are always asking to see your reel, so they can see what you look like on film. It's time to start making wise choices for your business, so you can stay in business!

CHAPTER 4

DEFINING THE RESUME

The Other Side Of Your Calling Card

An acting resume doesn't look like your standard job resume. Casting directors, agents and managers could be credited for creating the standard acting resume, which has not always been accessible to actors. Rarely would you know if you were making mistakes to your resume unless you worked behind the scenes. To help keep you on track as you create your acting resume, and prevent you from doing any damage to your career, I have created the following resume guide. Remember, this is just a guide. Be sure to always follow the advice of your agent or manager first.

- **Start with your name.** This may seem simple enough, but I mention it because I've seen people leave their names off of their resume! Your name should always be included on your resume! If you end up being too difficult to find, casting directors will stop looking for you. Your name should be centered at the top of the resume, in at least a 14-to-16-point font size, to help casting directors see it clearly. You will also want to make sure the font you pick is legible. You don't want to make it too difficult to read.

- **Have a contact phone number.** Duh! If you don't have an agent or manager, you will still want to put down your personal contact phone number so industry professionals can reach you. If you do have an agent or manager, put down his or her name and contact information. Stay clear, however, from including any other personal information on your resume, such as a home address, social security number, and so on - although it's okay to include an email address. Casting will not need your personal information until you have booked the job. It is not necessary to give that information to anyone until then. If you are looking for representation and do not currently live in Los Angeles, you will want to get an LA-based telephone number with a 213, 323, 310, or 818 area code. You don't need an actual phone line. An LA-based voicemail will do the trick, giving the agent, manager, or casting director the perception that you live here. It will also give you the opportunity to submit yourself for representation, until you decide to move to the West Coast.

- **Include your personal statistics.** Directly below the contact number, I recommend putting your personal statistics on your resume, such as height, weight, eye color, and hair color. You want the casting director to have an idea of what they're getting before they meet you in person. While I have heard arguments on both sides, I always think it helps to share this information. After all, I don't think it helps you as an artist if you get called in to audition for a role that requires someone six feet tall, when you're only five foot five. Yes, you got in; but you won't book the job, no matter how great you are. I would prefer the casting director call you in for something you have a legitimate shot of booking. CD's are way too smart. Don't try to hide what you are selling; embrace it.

- **Create a header—then organize your resume into three columns.** The name, contact number, and personal statistics discussed above should be considered your header, placed at the top of your resume. Once your header is in place, you will start listing your acting credits. These should be organized into three parallel, vertical columns, each of which is discussed in detail below.

1. **Column one: credits by genre.** The first column should be organized by genre: film, television, commercials, theater, training, and special skills. Since Los Angeles is a film town, your resume should always start with your film credits. If you don't have a lot of film credits, you will want to combine film and television into one category, which will give the perception that you have more film/television credits than you actually do.

JOHN SMITH
(310) 555-1212

Height:	6'2"	Hair:	Black
Weight:	175	Eyes:	Blue

Film/Television
Mission Impossible III
The Ghost Whisperer

Commercials
Conflicts available upon request

Theater
Harvey

Training
The Audition Room

Special Skills
Basketball, baseball, ice skating, golf, improv. Accents: British, Scottish, Southern.

2.   **Column two:** Billing. In column two, you will write the billing you received for that particular project, listed in column one. Casting directors want to know what kind of experience you've had in front of the camera. Billing varies based on the project genre, as well as the deal that was negotiated between you and your agent, lawyer, and manager.

Film Billing. You will either be the lead in a film (example: Tom Cruise); a supporting player within the film (multiple scenes, but not the lead); or a principle player in the film (one scene, with a couple of lines). List the appropriate billing in column two parallel to the relevant credit listed on your resume. In column three, you will want to list the name of the distributor and/or director.

Television Billing. Billing for television differs greatly from that of films. You will never want to put featured billing on your resume. Most casting directors don't use the term "featured" anymore, because it is associated with extra work. Here is a list of television credits to choose from, and what distinguishes them individually:

Series Regular: A series regular is an actor who has booked a pilot. If you know the series *Friends*, Matthew Perry, David Schwimmer, Courtney Cox-Arquette, Jennifer Aniston, Lisa Kudrow, and Matt LeBlanc were all series regulars, on weekly.

Special Guest Star: This billing is usually reserved for celebrity clientele, negotiated between the agent or lawyer, and casting director.

Recurring Guest Star: The lead, appearing on the same show more than one time.

Guest Star: The lead in the show.

Co-Star: A supporting player in the show. There is the possibility of one scene, or a couple of lines.

Recurring (also known as the recurring co-star): If you are a co-star and have been on the same show more than once, write *recurring* on your resume. Let the casting director assume you were a guest star. In column three, you will want to list the network and/or director.

Commercial Billing

As an actor, you will always want to let ad agencies know if you have a conflict, which refers to appearances you have booked in commercials for products that might conflict with competing products. For example, if you booked a Coke commercial and have an audition tomorrow for Pepsi, that would be a conflict. Therefore, you will not be able to audition and book the Pepsi commercial. Let ad agencies know about any conflicts you may have. You don't, however, need to list them on your resume. Just put down the following:

Commercials
Conflicts available upon request

Even if you don't have any commercial conflicts, the perception is that you do, which is a good thing. Clarify in the audition room if you do have an actual conflict, but don't let the casting director know that you've never booked a commercial.

Theater Billing. For theater, you will want to add the character name in the billing column. Most casting directors know the size of the role based on the character. A common mistake actors will make is to list both the character name and the size of the role (such as lead or supporting). In my experience, that clutters the resume. Don't be a pack-rat. Also, don't forget to add the name of the theatre and/or theatre company in column three. Here's an example:

Theater
Harvey   Elwood P. Dowd   Getz Theatre

Training. Training is not only important for your resume, but important for your career. Casting directors want to know the following:

1. Type of class
2. Teacher
3. City where you took the class

Your resume should be well rounded with both comedy and drama. If you have a lot of sitcom, stand-up, and improv experience on your resume, you probably won't get called in to audition for the one-hour drama. If you have a lot of one-hour drama credits on your resume, chances are you won't be auditioning for a lot of half-hour comedies. Try to have a balance of both, so you have the opportunity to audition for both.

You may also want to list any degrees you may have received, and the school, college, or university you went to. You may add the year you graduated, but if you think you still look young enough to play high school, don't post the year you graduated college.

Training
| The Casting Playhouse | Jason Buyer | Los Angeles, CA |
| B.A. in Theater | Columbia College | 1995 |

Special Skills. Anything that makes you unique or different within your market, put it down. This information is extremely helpful when casting for commercials. Your special skills may end up being the reason you get called in to audition in the first place. It's amazing what some people will get called in to do, based on the special skills section of their resume. Remember, you don't have to be a professional, you just have to be able to perform the skill when asked in the audition room.

Special Skills

Ice skating, fly fishing, horseback riding, golf, basketball, rollerblading, guitar, improv, stage combat, driving stick shift, crying on cue. Dialects: British, Southern, Irish.

Here's an example of what your completed resume should look like:

JOHN SMITH
(310) 555-1212

| Height: | 6'2" | | Hair: | Black |
| Weight: | 175 | | Eyes: | Blue |

Film/Television

| Mission Impossible III | Lead | Paramount Pictures/ JJ Abrams |
| The Ghost Whisperer | Co-star | Dir: Mel Damski/CBS |

Commercials
Conflicts available upon request

Theatre

| Harvey | Elwood P. Dowd | Geffen Playhouse |

Training

| The Audition Room | Jason Buyer | Los Angeles, CA |

Special Skills
Basketball, baseball, ice skating, golf, improv. Accents: British, Southern, Irish.

Without being a casting assistant first, I would never have had the opportunity to be a casting director and cast my own projects. I also wouldn't have had the opportunity to learn from other people's mistakes. For example:

<u>Film/TV</u>
The Price Is Right   Contestant   CBS

The Price Is Right is not a television credit that you would want to put on the back of your acting resume. The Price is Right, although on television, is not acting. The role of the contestant is not a role you were cast in, nor a character you tried to portray on screen. Be smart about how you are representing yourself, and your business. In other words, stop being stupid!

Ladder of Opportunity

An actor must go through many different stages before booking a job. Let's start with feature films. Several leading roles may have already been offered out to name talent, which means that an actor or actress may be attached to the project. Although each production differs, the majority of the supporting or principle roles in feature films are cast a month or two before shooting starts. Unless the casting director is already familiar with your work, the first level you must go through is what is known as the pre-read. A pre-read is a reading or audition with the actor and the casting director. If you do well in your pre-read, you would then move on and be called back to producers. At the producer session, all of the producers, the director, the writers, and casting director will sit in. If your producer session goes well, you may be called back again (and again) to screen test with the star of the film. A screen test is an audition with another actor that is recorded on camera. This is also known as a chemistry read. It's extremely important for the film's team to see how you look on film, as well as how you interact with the lead. Studios will not conduct a screen test for smaller roles, and a majority of the supporting or principle roles in feature films will be cast after finding our leads.

Television works a little differently, and each genre within it has its own particular process. Let's start with the comedy genre, or thirty-minute episodic programming. A sitcom and single-camera comedy are shot on a five-day shooting schedule, which means that a casting director doesn't have a lot of time to audition new talent. There will be one casting session scheduled, with the possibility of a second session, if casting can't find what they need. The schedule is extremely tight: Production receives a script at the beginning of the week, and the episode is taped or shot by the end of the week. Actors may be called in to audition for a pre-read with the casting director, possibly get called back for the producers, and if it all goes well, book the job. The producers and director will make the final decision on who gets cast. Note: Larger roles usually require network approval before being cast.

One-hour dramas and dramedies are on an eight-day episodic shooting schedule. Because there is more time, a casting director can schedule multiple casting sessions with the producers if needed. This could be good news for actors looking to audition! Again, larger roles usually require network approval before being cast.

A television pilot is somewhat different. A pilot is the first episode of any new show, and is on an eleven day shooting schedule. Casting directors have more time (sometimes months) to cast the leads or series regulars for pilots. Because of that, they tend to read more actors. Remember, a casting directors' biggest nemesis is time. They simply cannot read or audition as many actors as they would like, no matter what kind of project it is, and no matter how right you might be for it. A casting directors' job is to simply make sure that the project gets cast.

If you have an audition for a new pilot, you will more than likely start out pre-reading with the casting director, unless they already know your work. If the casting director is familiar with what you can do in the audition room, you may end up going straight to producers. If you do end up pre-reading and it goes well, you will be called back to read for the producers, writers, director, and casting director. You may be called back multiple times, before they decide whether or not they would like to bring you to the next level – studio. The studio session includes all of the studio executives, writers, director, producers, and casting director. During the studio session, contract negotiations will begin. Your pilot contract is negotiated between your agent or lawyer and the business affairs associate assigned to the project. Contract negotiations must be finalized before auditioning for the final stage in the pilot process, network. Why does your contract need to be signed before going into a network read? The answer is simple. If your agent or manager knew that you were the choice for the role, your agent or manager would ask for more money. If your contract is not signed before the network test, you will not be able to audition for the network executives. In essence, failing to sign your contract is equivalent to passing on the project. The network session is the final stage of pilot casting, and will include the casting director, producers, writers, director, studio executives, and network executives. You will likely read with the star of the show. In all, there could be up to 25 people in the room.

You should know relatively soon after testing whether or not you booked the series. The actor will either be placed on hold (yes, more waiting), released from the job, or book the job. There's also the possibility that no one booked the job. If the network executives didn't respond to any of the choices, casting directors would then start the casting process all over again. CD's have to get the project cast, or they could lose their job – it's that simple.

It's Not Easy Being Green

An actor who doesn't have a lot of acting experience is known in the industry as being "green." Casting directors and other industry professionals use the term to describe the level of talent—or, rather, the lack thereof. An actor who is "green" can be a casting director's best defense for not moving an actor forward during the casting process. That's not to say the casting director won't bring the actor in for a different role or a different project entirely; that's certainly still possible, but probably for a smaller role.

Being "green" in the audition room and being "green" based on the limited number of credits on your resume is never a good thing. But having too many credits might actually hurt your chances. Remember, the primary job of an agent or manager is to be able to mold and shape your career as an actor. That's not possible when you have too many credits listed on your resume. You don't want to give off the perception that you've done everything. Who will want to work with you then? Be careful and picky about how you sell yourself and what ends up on your resume. When the resume becomes too cluttered (especially if you don't have an agent or manager representing you), it becomes much harder for anyone to want to represent you. Don't be "green" – although a light shade of lime probably wouldn't hurt you.

Smart Billing

I can't tell you how many poorly prepared resumes I have come across during my twelve years of casting. Making mistakes on your resume can end up hurting your chances of being seen by those who matter most.

You need to make sure you proofread your resume carefully, and have someone else you trust check it as well. You wouldn't go into a job interview with a resume that had grammatical errors and column and spacing mistakes, would you? That's the point: You need to treat every audition as if you are going in for a job interview!

If you don't know exactly how to put together an acting resume, ask; it's better than being wrong, especially with billing. Billing errors are the most common mistakes actors make on their acting resume. Again, you will need to make the necessary changes to your resume based on the genre, or type of project. Let's end this vicious cycle and get these resumes compatible for the casting director!

We talked in Chapter 2 about the importance of selling a specific type, or product. Continue to sell your specific types; but be careful that your resume doesn't pigeonhole you as only being able to play small roles. You don't want to be pigeonholed as an extra or background actor. This is why you should never put extra work on your resume.

Do you know the expression, "There are no small roles, only small actors"? As an actor, you will need to be smart about what you put down on your resume, especially for smaller roles.

For film, it's principle billing. For TV, it's co-star billing. For a soap opera, it's a day player or "under 5." Booking a smaller role is a great credit to your resume, especially if you are just starting out; but remember that you don't want your career to be solely based on playing smaller roles. Here's a story to illustrate my point.

A client of mine was fortunate enough to be signed with a well-respected talent agency in Los Angeles. He had booked four co-stars on several different episodic television shows. That was a good start, but his agent was concerned that he would be pigeonholed as a co-star actor, not worthy of being called in for any leading or guest-starring roles. So what did the agent do? The agent decided to change the billing on all four co-stars listed on his resume to guest-stars, thus making him the lead in each episode. My client was extremely nervous about this. "What if I get caught?" he asked. Well, unfortunately, he did get caught. The casting director ended up calling the talent agent directly to let them know that there was a billing error on his resume, an error that the agent was already aware of since he was the one that created it. The agent said that it was his assistant that was responsible for the mistake, since she is the one who makes changes to the clients' resumes. The agent said he would change it immediately to the correct billing, co-star. Of course, the agent never did. Since the resume was already in full circulation, CD's slowly began to call my client in for guest-starring roles, or leads. The exact same week my client was busted for embellishing his resume, he booked his first guest-starring role. Now that the actor had a legitimate guest-starring credit on his resume, his agent was comfortable changing the previous four "guest-stars" back to co-star credits. As for the actor? He is now a recurring guest-star on a major one-hour drama on a major network.

As unfair (and wrong) as it may be, that story makes sense. No matter what the genre, if you've never done it, casting directors will just assume that you probably can't. If you've never been a lead in a movie or a guest-star on a television show, why should they believe that you can be a lead in a movie or a guest-star on a television show? Just because you *want* to? That reason is simply not good enough.

A client of mine who has been unable to get called in for larger roles recently consulted with me and expressed her concern over the twelve co-starring roles listed on her resume.

Based on this information, it's safe to say that my client knows how to book a small role on an episodic show. Now ask yourself this question: If you were casting a guest-starring role on a major NBC show, would you bring her in to audition? The truth is, she would not be called in for any guest-starring role, because she has never booked a guest-star. She would definitely be called in for the co-star, however. I know she can do that!

Depending on the project, the first several jobs you book on television will probably be a co-star. With that in mind, here's how you can avoid being a co-star actor:

1. **Stop auditioning for co-starring or principle roles.** Tell your agent or manager that you no longer want to be considered for smaller roles. They will stop submitting you for them, and pretty soon, you won't be going out for them. The only problem is that it's possible you won't be going out for anything. I don't recommend this, although it still remains an option. For young actors, especially those that are just getting started, it's a very risky move. The industry has changed dramatically in the past ten years and any opportunity to audition is usually a good opportunity, even if it's for a smaller role.

2. **Don't put it on your resume.** Continue to audition for principle and co-starring roles, book the job, but don't list the credit. This will keep the number of co-stars to a minimum. Again, it's an option, but not one I recommend. I think you should always list your most recent bookings on your resume, so you stay current and active in the industry. It's important for casting directors to know that the last job you booked was recent, and not

from ten years ago. You can get rusty in this business, and even if you aren't, not listing your most current credits will make it will look like you are.

3.   **Revolving co-star/principle cycle.** Try this! Book the job, listing your most recent credit on your resume. Limit your resume to four co-star/principle credits at one time. If you book a fifth co-star, take one off, removing your oldest co-starring/principle credit first. This cycle keeps you current, and allows you, the actor, the possibility of being called in for a much larger role down the road.

Remember, it doesn't do you much good to keep old credits on your resume, so don't be afraid to remove them. If you have already booked several guest-starring roles, don't worry about how many co-stars you have on your resume. You can list all of them if you would like. This resume technique is for the actor who has yet to be the lead in an episodic series, pilot, or feature film.

Too much drama/comedy

If you have a lot of comedy on your resume, such as stand-up, improv, half-hour sitcom or half-hour comedy single camera, you probably won't be called in to audition for a lot of one-hour dramas. If your resume primarily consists of dramatic work, you probably won't be called in to audition for too many comedies. Ideally, you will want to have a mixed bag on your resume, with both comedic and dramatic elements. If one of these genres happens to be your niche, however, then this technique would not apply.

Spoiler Alert: The Resume Paper

When I first started casting, I would receive all kinds of pictures and resumes. Back in the day, actors would rubber cement their resume to the back of the headshot, staple the resume on all sides, and cut around the edges of the resume to fit the picture. Apparently, there was a big fear that the resume would fly off of the headshot. It looked horrible. Although 90 percent of all casting is now done online, actors will always need a hard-copy picture and resume, especially walking into a casting session. Casting directors always want something tangible in their hands. This leaves 10 percent of all casting directors requesting hard-copy submissions, while a few CD's are asking for both electronic and hard copy submissions.

Today, the biggest talent agencies in Los Angeles - CAA, William Morris/Endeavor (WME), ICM, UTA, Innovative Artists, Gersh, Paradigm, etc, do things a bit differently. The resume is centered and lined up with the picture, then attached with a center staple on top and bottom, holding the resume intact. The sides and bottom of the resume are no longer cut to fit the picture.

Heaven forbid you don't get called in to audition because you cut your resume to fit the picture - or didn't cut your resume at all. As actors, I want you to think big. If the biggest companies aren't cutting the resume to fit the picture, you should think about taking the same approach. Most importantly, if your agent or manager still wants you to cut your resume to fit the picture, by all means do it! It isn't worth the argument. But no more rubber cement. That's the good news!

A-List Agencies & Managers

I can't imagine why anyone would be in this industry if they didn't love it. My personal goal for you is simple: To have a long-lasting career doing what you love to do. It's about working, and getting the opportunity to work—and, along the way, if you become known for your work, so be it. This book is designed to give you, the actor, a business model for reaching your goals, both in and out of the audition room. However, sometimes, you can't do it alone.

With more than 200 SAG-franchised agencies and over 700 managers in Los Angeles, it is vital that you find representation that will be able to move your career forward. Signing with an agency that doesn't have a good reputation turns you into an actor who doesn't have a lot of talent. My best advice on representation? Do your research. Is your agent able to get you out for leading or guest-starring roles? What about co-stars? Does your agent currently have any clients on a series? The more your representation can do, the more auditions you will have.

I have put together a list of characteristics I believe make up an A-list talent agency.

A-List agents:

- Submit for guest-starring roles. (You want to be the lead, so you need to go out for leading roles. Again, 90 percent of casting is now done online.)

- Pitch verbally to casting, producers, and directors. *(Is your agent getting on the phone and pitching you for a particular role? They need to be.)*

- Send out your demo reel. *(Sometimes, if you are unavailable for the pre-read, a demo reel can be sent in its place. Casting directors have also made straight offers based on demo reels.)*

- Push for pre-read appointments. *(A CD's worst fear is being embarrassed in front of the director and producers. No embarrassment if it's just you, the actor, and casting director.)*

- Use personal relationships to open doors. *(Who you know, as well as who they know.)*

- Ask for client feedback. *(Feedback is when your agent or manager calls the CD to find out how you did in the room, after you have auditioned.)*

- Pitch clients for general meetings. *(A general is a meeting between you and the industry professional, set up by your agent or manager, usually during the slower months. It can be scheduled at any time, but usually before pilot and episodic seasons.)*

- Ask for better billing. *(The actor will usually know what type of role they are auditioning for before they go in. Billing can be negotiated, especially the order in which the actor is placed on the card, the front or back end when credits role.)*

- Ask for more money. *(Casting directors begin with a budget. It always makes the CD look good if they are saving the production company money. Based on the casting budget, any amount of money that has not been used towards the booking of an actor can be saved, or applied to a more expensive actor, if necessary.)*

- Represent high-profile, working actors. *(The agency gets them in the door, sometimes without even being pitched. Logo casting.)*

- Ask for talent perks, such as a larger trailer. *(If there is a larger trailer on the set and no one is using it, why not have your client use it? Sometimes, however, it's not worth the fight.)*

- Develop and package clients. *(Attaching a client to a particular project so it has a better chance of being financed and sold.)*

- Get you more auditions. *(This one speaks for itself.)*

- Have neatly displayed submission presentations. *(Again, most casting is now done online, but some casting directors still do it the old-fashioned way. How does your picture look when submitted via messenger? Is there a typed cover letter? Did your agency separate the headshots by character, with a paperclip or Post-it for easy sorting? Or is the character name scribbled on the picture? How does the submission packet come across?)*

- Move careers forward. *(A partnership to build your business, turning your talent into a career.)*

- Get you more auditions. *(Yes, I said this before. It's worth repeating.)*

A-List managers:

Have the same responsibilities as an A-List agent. (But there are a couple of things you'll want to be sure they're doing for you now.)

- Should always try to find you, the client, an agent. *(To do this, they should use the personal relationships they currently have.)*

- Should always be pitching you verbally over the phone, for any role, especially for pre-read appointments with the casting director. *(Since managers represent fewer clients than an agent, it allows them to spend more time on the phone, pitching all of their clients.)*

- Negotiate without negotiating. *(Technically, a manager cannot ask for more money when negotiating a booking or contract, but many of them still do. This is why it is crucial to have a solid relationship between your agent and manager.)*

- Should always be able to reinvent you, the client. *(However, you don't need a manager in order to reinvent your career. You can reinvent yourself with a career makeover. It is up to your management team to build the foundation for your future. You have to be open to selling something else, or changing your product if necessary.)*

- The standard commission for an agent is 10 percent of what the client books. A manager will make 15 percent of what the client books. Commission is always negotiable when you are dealing with high-end celebrity clientele who are bringing in millions of dollars per project.

Agents and managers can, and will, take less commission in these circumstances.

Yes, You Need A Manager

Managers weren't as popular a decade ago as they are today. Most actors have managers, whether or not they have careers that actually need to be managed. Having another group, team, or individual pitching to get you in the audition room is priceless. After all, giving away 25 percent (10 percent to the agent, 15 percent to the manager) of something is better than giving away 0 percent of nothing. Just get in the room. The money will follow.

CHAPTER 5

BOOKING THE JOB

Style of the Show

It is so important to know the show, or genre, as you prepare your audition material. I recommend following what's on the page, and using the writing blueprint that has been provided for you – the script.

With all auditions, you should receive the character description, or breakdown, from your agent or manager before going in to the audition room. The breakdown will give you insight into the character. Tweak your performance based on the character description and individual writing style of the show. It's not about what you want to bring to the material; it's what the writers, producers, casting director, and director want you to bring to the material, based on what's written on the page.

So, what if you don't have the luxury of getting the breakdown before your audition? Don't worry. Just follow these helpful hints and you'll succeed with flying colors.

Read the Material

Sounds simple enough, right? You'd be surprised. With so many different types of shows out there, it can be difficult to differentiate among them. Remember, there are many genres and styles to choose from.

Spacing. There are only two genres with script formats that are currently double-spaced: half-hour sitcoms and soap operas.

1.   Half-Hour Sitcoms
      An example of this would be "Two and a Half Men".
2.   Soap Operas
      An example of this would be "Days of Our Lives"

You should be able to tell the difference between a sitcom and a soap opera just by reading the material. Even though these are the only two genres that are double-spaced, they read very differently.

With half-hour sitcoms, the dialogue is double-spaced and centered on the page. With a soap opera, the dialogue is also double-spaced, but is usually placed on the left side of the page, allowing the actor to write down his or her specific blocking or script notes towards the center or right side of the page.

What does this mean for you, the actor? It means that every other genre will be single-spaced: Half-Hour Comedy, Single Camera, Dramedy, One-Hour Drama, and Feature Films (Drama and Comedy) Here are some examples:

- Half-Hour Comedy, Single Camera
  "The Office" or "30 Rock"

- One-Hour Drama
  "CSI" or "Criminal Minds"

- Dramedy
  "Desperate Housewives" or "Glee"

- Feature Film, Drama
  "The Lovely Bones"

- Feature Film, Comedy
  "The Hangover"

- Half-Hour Comedy, Sitcom (Double-Spaced)
  "How I Met Your Mother" or "Rules of Engagement"

- Soap Opera (Double-Spaced)
  "Days of Our Lives"

On paper, the first five genres look exactly the same, which certainly can be confusing when the actor is trying to prepare. It's important to emphasize these differences in the audition room. In the next chapter, we will discuss the formula for each individual genre.

How Great Do You Want To Be?

I never want you to just hope for the best. As an actor, you need a plan or strategy, and hope is not a strategy! You have an amazing opportunity to shine in front of the people that matter most. Don't settle for anything less when it comes to your career. You deserve the best, and you deserve to book the job - NOW. Audition technique is a process. The real work starts after you know your lines. Memorization will give you confidence, but is not part of the formula that I teach.

The Callback Means They Like You

My clients often ask me what they should be doing differently in the callback. The answer is simple: DON'T DO ANYTHING DIFFERENTLY! I'm not sure if it's just because actors have self-destructive tendencies, but as a teacher, I give you permission to stop shooting yourself in the foot. You deserve success. Remember, the callback is the best feedback you can get. If you get called back, the casting director isn't looking for you to do anything differently, or to take your scene in a new direction— only to take direction, if asked. Listen to what they want you to do, before doing it.

When I was casting at MGM, I would schedule fourteen to sixteen actors for our producer session, pre-read forty to fifty actors, and call back one or two—and that's only if someone dropped out or was unavailable to attend the producer session. Consider it a blessing that you got called in to audition in the first place. Don't risk the job by making new choices for the callback. Unfortunately, an actor has very little control in the beginning stages of his or her career. Keep your reading fresh, but don't change what we liked.

What about wearing the same outfit to your callback? My opinion is that it's not necessary. Your clothes didn't get the callback, you did! I think it's funny when an actor is called back two or three days later and is wearing the same outfit they wore to the pre-read appointment. It's more important that you come into the audition room looking presentable, dressed parallel to how the character would dress (based on the breakdown). You'll also want to avoid perfume or cologne—you never know who happens to be allergic. And for goodness sake, take a shower! Not having showered and stinking up the room is a surefire way of not being called back—ever.

Mandatory Websites & How You Represent Yourself

Several websites allow actors to take proactive steps in their careers, even if they don't have representation. That's right: You will be submitting yourself until you are fortunate enough to get an agent or manager. Let's start with one of the most important websites for actors: Actors Access (www.actorsaccess.com). We've talked a lot about Breakdown Services in past chapters, which owns Actors Access. As a reminder, here's what Breakdown Services does:

- Puts out the Agency and Casting Director Guides, seasonally.

- Breaks down each script by character, including age, ethnicity, and prototype, if available.

- Releases casting notices to the agents, managers, and actors who have registered on Actors Access, which is a division of Breakdown Services.

Actors Access is a valuable website for actors who are looking to submit themselves for potential jobs. Although many casting notices are omitted from this site, it still gives the actor the opportunity to submit themselves for low-budget and independent projects. It is up to the casting director if they would like to release the breakdown, or audition information to the agents, the agents and managers, or the agents, managers, and actors on Actors Access. Most of the SAG and AFTRA audition notices are released through the Breakdowns, and not Actors Access. This information would then be accessible to only theatrical agents and managers. Occasionally, however, there is some trickle down to the Actors Access website.

LA Casting (www.lacasting.com) and Now Casting (www.nowcasting.com) are similar to Actors Access, giving actors the opportunity to submit themselves for roles they feel they may be right for, based on the online audition notice and character description. Both websites are extremely useful tools for actors who are looking to take pro-active steps in their careers. Actors no longer have to wait for representation to be considered, although having representation certainly helps.

Electronic Submissions

Electronic submissions didn't exist twelve years ago when I first began casting. Today, more than 90 percent of all casting is done electronically. The online process allows for a quicker turnaround for casting directors as well as agents and managers. It also makes submitting actors easier and certainly more cost-effective, not to mention all of the trees that are being saved.

There are, however, some faults to the electronic submission system. Because agents and managers only have to click a mouse in order to submit their clients, casting becomes more and more inundated with choices, forcing CD's to pay less attention to the smaller agencies, and more attention towards submissions from agencies with which they are most familiar. There are some casting directors who are unwilling to adapt to the new electronic system, while others continue to ask for both (hard copy and electronic), which then ends up taking more time to submit effectively.

Electronic submissions could have the potential to be extremely effective if everyone used them. Significant progress has been made, however. The system still requires the user to click on the mouse in order to not only submit, but change pictures or review an actor's resume. You wouldn't think that this would be a big deal, but imagine if you are looking through three thousand submissions to cast just one role. Overall, the online casting system that has been created by Gary Marsh and Breakdown Services is an excellent one, and has revolutionized the entertainment industry.

I was recently hired to cast a role in an independent feature film which is now making its way through the festival circuit. I was looking to cast a 35-40 year old Caucasian male to play the role of a parole officer. As a casting director, it was my job to make sure that I was giving the director and producers the best available choices. I knew that I would have plenty of actors to choose from, but was concerned over the budget - a $250.00 flat fee for one day's work. I began making my lists, and was prepping to release the breakdown on Breakdown Services, Now Casting, LA Casting, and Actors Access. I was also accepting hard-copy submissions for the role.

To my amazement, by the end of my first day I had received more than two thousand electronic submissions—more than half of those within the first hour. An additional 2,500 submissions came in after I had already cast the role, plus I had a mail bin full of hard-copy submissions that, unfortunately, I never had the chance to open.

I had the opportunity to pre-read fifty actors, calling back the best ten for my producers. My casting session couldn't have gone better, and I was thrilled with the producer's top choice. To my surprise, they ended up going with an actor who physically fit the part, but probably gave one of the worst auditions. As I always like to say, you don't have to be the best actor in the room, just sell something people want. (Although being the best certainly helps!) The director, who was not present at the time of the producer session, was able to see and cast the actor he wanted from tape. Although he agreed that the reading didn't go well, he was confident that he could work with the actor, pulling out what he needed from his performance. He could not, however, change how he envisioned the look of the character.

CHAPTER 6

THE FORMULA

The formula is my step-by-step approach to the audition technique process, using all of the necessary elements and guidelines an actor will need to succeed in the audition room. I have based the formula on more than a dozen years of casting experience, giving the entire creative team—not just the casting director, but also the director, producers and writers what they want.

There are five main rules an actor needs to follow in order to master the formula. These rules may change slightly based on the type of show or genre the actor is auditioning for, but for the most part, they remain the same for each. In order:

1. **Breathing.** It sounds simple, but it's crucial. For any comedy, the audience needs to catch up to the joke. As soon as your audience starts to wait for the jokes, the show is no longer funny and your audience loses interest. For drama, the audience needs to catch up to the action of the scene. Again, you lose your audience as soon as your scene stops moving forward. Remember, in the audition room, casting directors don't have the luxury of editing. Move your scene forward by taking a breath in, and exhaling and talking though your line until you reach the end of the sentence. Repeat.

   Exercise: Grab a script, book or newspaper, and practice breathing through your lines. Take a breath in, and breathe out (exhale) and talk all the way through the line until you get to the end of the sentence. Don't stop mid-sentence and break up the line to take a breath. Don't think about where you would like to add emphasis. It's no longer about what you want to do with the text, but rather what the writers want you to do and what they are asking you to do. In other words, keep your scene moving! Continue by repeating this step – take a breath in, and exhale and talk all the way through the line. Don't hold your breath, or take multiple breaths throughout your lines—that's just going to slow down your scene. Breathe out and talk through the line. Take another breath in when you begin your next sentence.

Why do you need to do this? As an audience, our attention spans are minimal, and your audience will tune you out if they lose interest. When you audition, you have about two minutes in the audition room to make a true connection with the casting director, so the actor doesn't have time to break up lines. Every time you stop, you break the continuity of the scene, and prevent yourself from developing a connection in the room. Learn to keep your scene moving so you can stay connected to the reader. Don't get me wrong: Every actor breaks up lines, but keep it to a minimum so your audience remains engaged.

2.   **Punctuation**

Adding your own punctuation to the script also slows you down in the audition room. Again, give the writers what they want, and follow what's on the page. Treat your script as the writers' blueprint. Breaking up your lines or adding your own punctuation can prevent you from moving your scene forward, which stops the action (drama), or prevents you from hitting the jokes (comedy). Follow the punctuation on the page. If there is a period, stop. If there is a comma, pause. If there is an exclamation point, get louder!

Every statement, 100 percent of the time, should have a downward inflection at the end. If your statement doesn't have a downward inflection at the end of the line, there's a good chance that it will sound like a question, or sound like you have more to say. It doesn't matter how high your pitch is at the beginning or even in the middle of your statement; by the time you reach the end, your inflection should have gone down, as if you are finished with that particular thought or statement.

Questions are different: 90 percent of all questions will go up at the end, leaving only 10 percent of all questions to go down, and that can be confusing.

How do you know when you should be going up towards the end of the line and when you should be going down towards the end of the line? The numbers don't lie. As a first step, follow the percentages when you are breaking down your text. There's a good chance your question is going to go up, simply based on the formula – questions going up 90 percent of the time. As a second step, see what follows. If a statement follows your question, it's a better choice for your question to go up, since all of your statements will end up going down. Casting directors want highs and lows within the text – makes it interesting.

Remember, the more your voice goes down at the end of your lines, the lower the energy will be in your scene - great for drama, but not very helpful for comedy. You certainly don't want to fall flat in the audition room. The more you go up at the end of your lines, the higher the energy is within your scene. That's great for comedy, but will probably be too big for drama. The choice to go up or down should be based on the genre as well as what has been written before and after the line. As a third step, say your question out loud with up and down inflections. Which is the better choice? Which one is real?

Example:

Really? I didn't know that.

The best choice based on the formula is to go up on "*Really?*", and to go down on "*I didn't know* that". Make sure you bring in both the high and low levels in this line. High and up on the question, and down and low for your statement.

3. **Thoughts:** One of the more difficult components of the formula is learning the thought process, and allowing your audience (CD) to see and connect to what you are thinking before you respond. I will teach you how to apply and use thoughts correctly within your text. The rule is simply this:

    Your text or dialogue is your direct response to what you are thinking. Show us what you are thinking before you respond. The moment before you begin speaking is what is known as "the thought."

    Actors who don't know or don't understand the formula will resort back to their instincts, which will be correct 50 percent of the time. That means that if your plan is to rely on your instincts, expect to be wrong half of the time. Those are not great odds when you are trying to book a job. As an actor, it is extremely important to back up your choices and not leave them to chance. Having a clear thought before you speak allows you to do this. Thoughts need to be in the form of dialogue, for your head. In other words, you won't be saying your thought out loud in the audition room; you will be thinking your thought, just prior to responding with the line of dialogue.

    Not only does having the right thought allow the actor to say the line correctly, but it also allows the actor to bring in a physical moment just before the actor responds. Yes, having a thought does have multiple purposes!

Are you the type of actor that looks at a line of dialogue, and says it out loud 20 or 30 different ways before making a choice? Have you backed up your choices in the past, or do you just trust your instincts? Your choices may sound right, but is it right? Hoping that you picked the right choice won't work. You'll probably never audition as much as you would like, so don't leave it up to chance when you get the opportunity. After all, it's never a good idea to say your lines *wrong*. If you've done your homework correctly, the thought will be in your head prior to responding.

Start asking yourself what you are thinking *before* you respond. I don't want you to just say the lines; that's acting. As a casting director and acting coach, I never want to see you acting. You need to be real, allowing your audience (CD) to see why you are saying what has been written on the page. Just like in everyday life, you say something to someone, a thought gets registered in their head, and then they say something back to you in response (dialogue). Think of your script as the answer key; you just need to come in with two main questions.

1. "Why am I saying this?" (intention)
2. "What am I thinking that gets me to respond?" (thought)

Scene study allows actors to talk about what is happening in the script, which may be useful once you have booked the job; but it can be considered unusable when prepping for an audition, and is not part of the formula. You have a very small amount of time to connect to the casting director in an audition. You won't have enough time to show them your "character." The character is you. As I tell all of my clients, "It doesn't matter what your character ate for breakfast." That information will never help you say your dialogue correctly in the audition room. You may have to use certain characteristics to help sell your "character," but always allow us to connect to who you are first. Save the majority of your character development for when you have actually booked the job.

Having a thought and backing up your choices allows the actor to be in the "now" or in the moment at all times. In other words, thoughts allow the actor to be in the scene as it's happening. Talking about your scene doesn't allow the actor to be in the "now." Talking about your scene allows you to *talk about your scene* - and talk, and talk, and talk some more. You can talk about your scene until you are blue in the face, it still doesn't allow the actor to be in the "now". Talking about your scene doesn't get you in the game, it gets you to the sidelines so you can watch the game, and report on it later. I don't want you talking about what the character is doing or feeling. The character is you, so make sure *you* stay in the scene.

Here are some examples to help you as you learn how to create your own thoughts. The first column represents scene study, while in the second column, you'll see corresponding words, in thought form.

Talking about your scene (Scene Study)	Being in your scene (Creating dialogue)
He's angry.	"NOOOOOO!!!"
She's sad.	"That's terrible."
She's really happy to see him.	"Oh my god!"
He's depressed.	"I'm so upset."
She's surprised.	"I can't believe it!"

As you write down your thoughts, make sure to match the punctuation. For example, if your line is a statement, your thought will need to be a statement. If your line is a question, your thought will need to be in the form of a question – and don't forget the 90/10 rule with questions. Such preparation and awareness can make the difference between saying the line right and saying the line wrong.

Finally, when you are breaking down your material, imagine that you are the writer. In other words, try not to think like an actor. Stop talking about what's happening in your scene. Write down your thoughts for all of your lines, and ask yourself what you are thinking that gets you to respond. You should have a thought before every line. Does your thought make sense within your story? Is your thought simple dialogue that you have created for your head? Did you follow the punctuation on the paper? If you are able to answer "yes" to these questions, then you are well on your way to learning the formula.

4.   **Levels**

Adding levels will always make your scene more interesting and enjoyable to watch. Without levels, your scene becomes monotonous, general, and boring. Levels are broken down into three specific categories:

1.   Volume (loud/soft)
2.   Pitch (high/low)
3.   Pace (fast/slow)

As an actor, your voice is your instrument, and can be considered the most important asset you have. Varying your levels will help keep your audience on their toes, while allowing them to connect to your performance. Your levels must always adapt to the genre you are auditioning for. For example, if you are auditioning for a comedy, you may bring in more volume, pitch, and pace, since all comedies require more energy. For your dramatic work, your levels should be smaller and controlled.

Every actor has a level line. An actor is either over his or her level line, below his or her level line, or close to his or her level line. Your level line as an actor will change based on the genre you are auditioning for.

- **Over the level line.** Being over your level line simply means that you have broken the imaginary third wall, and your audience can now see you performing. In other words, we don't believe you. Being fake, not real, or over the top is a direct result of being over your level line. Stop acting.

- **Below the level line.** If you are below your level line, your performance is leaning toward the boring side, and you haven't brought in enough energy to save your scene. Although your performance is real, it probably won't be enough to get you called back.

- **Close to the level line.** The goal is to get as close as possible to your level line without going over it. This means that you are bringing the appropriate volume, pitch, and pace within your scene while staying true to the genre you are auditioning for. Keep this up, and I see a callback in your future.

Level Line Exercise

Pick two lines of dialogue from a recent script, sides, or monologue that you have been working on. Pick out one statement and one question, if possible. Create a thought for each of them, matching up the punctuation. In order to begin to understand each genre and the differences between them, try delivering the same line of dialogue for every genre listed below. You should be able to recognize and hear the differences. The levels in your voice will begin changing as you deliver your line or lines. Remember, you need to adapt your choices to the genre; don't expect the genre to adapt to you. (½ Hour Sitcom, ½ Hour Comedy Single-Camera, Dramedy, 1 Hour Drama, Feature Film)

5. **Keeping It Real**

    Casting directors are always looking for a connection in the audition room, based on your performance. Your best chance of providing that connection is to stay true to who you are. Again, we never want to see you acting. All your hard work up to this point doesn't mean anything unless we believe you and your performance. In other words, make us care. Don't bring in levels that are going to be too big, or thoughts that involuntarily break up the line; such errors go directly against the rules of the formula and will hurt you in the audition room. Remember, the character is *you*, and you are always enough. Incorporating yourself as part of any character will allow you to maintain a true performance. Most importantly, it should prevent you from accidently going over your level line.

6. **Number the Jokes**

    This rule only applies to the comedy genre:

    1/2-hour sitcom

    1/2-hour comedy; single camera

    Dramedy (jokes aren't as obvious)

    Feature film (comedy only)

    Comedies usually have two or three jokes per page. Can you find them? I consider every comedy to have two different types of jokes, each placed strategically within a story. They are:

    1.   Timing
    2.   Circumstance

A timing joke is just that – a joke based on it's delivery. The other type of joke is based on circumstance or the character relationships within the story, and may not be as obvious. I feel you need both types in order to execute any comedic material effectively.

The Formula – A Review

1.   Breathe through your lines

Take a breath in, and talk and exhale through your lines. This pushes your story forward.

2.   Punctuation

Follow the punctuation on the paper, and don't bring in your own. It's no longer about what you want to do, but rather what the writers want you to do.

3.   Thoughts

Everything on the sheet of paper (sides) is your direct response to what you are thinking. Casting directors need to see what you are thinking before you talk. Thoughts need to be in the form of dialogue for your head. Having a thought will allow you to not only say the line correctly, but allow you to have a physical moment before you talk (respond). You need both.

4.   Levels

Levels make your scene more enjoyable to watch. Every actor has a level line. The goal is to get as close as possible to your level line without going over it. Again, your level line will change based on what you are auditioning for (genre). Levels consist of volume, pitch, and pace.

5.   **Keep it real**

We never want to see you acting. Just be. At this stage in your career, it is not necessary for you to be playing characters. The best character you can play is you, one that your audience will have the easiest time connecting to. You may want to bring in characteristics of that character to help sell a type, but don't lose yourself in the process. The best selling point you have is simply to be yourself.

6.   **Number the jokes (comedy only)**

It's important to know where the jokes are. Sometimes you are setting up the other actor for the joke—and sometimes you have the joke, or punch line. Remember, there are two different types of jokes, and usually two or three to a page. To be successful, you will need to play both types.

Booking the Job - Where Do I Get My Sides?

If you already have representation, you will be able to get the breakdown and audition material from your agent or manager prior to going in to audition. If you are not represented by either an agent or manager, there are several other resources that you can use to retrieve your material. They include the following:

Now Casting (www.nowcasting.com)
Actors Access (www.actorsaccess.com)
Showfax (www.showfax.com)
Sides Express (www.sidesexpress.com)

Many of the above websites provide a network for actors to retrieve audition material. These websites also allow actors the capability to submit themselves electronically for a particular role on a particular project.

The Room – Own It!

Your audition begins the moment you walk into the audition room, not when you say your first line. You may give the reading of your life, but if you don't look the part, it won't go further. That's not to say that the CD wouldn't bring you in for a different role, something you are more appropriate for. Remember, the casting director has a direct link to what the producers and director are looking for, based on what was discussed in the casting concept meeting. Also, if a casting director wants you to do your scene over again, they will tell you before you leave the room; there is never a need to ask. Asking makes it look like you weren't pleased with your choices, not to mention how desperate it makes you look. You have one shot, so make the most of it. Don't forget: If you are lucky enough to get called back, by all means don't change what we originally loved! Remember why we called you back in the first place!

Dressing Parallel to the Part

When you are coming in to audition for a particular role, try not to dress exactly like the character. Rather, dress parallel to what you think the CD might be looking for. The character breakdown will give you some insight as to how you should dress for your audition; but you should avoid doing too much or going over the top with your wardrobe choice. The CD should be focused on your performance, not your outfit. Here's an example.

> *Audition: Law & Order: Los Angeles*
> *Role: Cop*
>
> *Breakdown*
> *Hard-Copy Submissions Only*
>
> *35-40 years old. Caucasian male, tough cop who plays by his own rules. 3-5 lines. Co-Star.*

The actors called in to audition for the cop will physically look the part. Casting will go through thousands of submissions and call in the actors who are actually dressed in a cop uniform, with the badge, hat, guns, etc., possibly leaning up against a squad car with a menacing look on their face. This is all portrayed in their headshot or thumbnail. It's okay to dress like this particular character in an 8-by-10 picture or thumbnail for a 3-to-5 line co-star. This is not a leading look, so if you use it, know that you are probably not going to be considered for the lead, or guest-star. The cop headshot is a co-star headshot, something to be used for smaller parts and similar roles. It will not work for a leading guest-starring role. Also, you don't want to walk into the audition room dressed as the cop - with the hat, badge, guns, etc. Dress parallel to what you think the CD is looking for. I would suggest wearing a button-down shirt with rolled-up sleeves and a loose tie the next time you are called in for this type of role.

Dressing Parallel to the Part—and the Exception

For commercials, it's okay to dress the part. This is frowned upon in the theatrical world, however. Dress parallel to the part, based on the commercial breakdown.

Avoid Props

As an actor, you should always get in the habit of bringing in your audition material, just in case you need it, and incorporating it into your scene. The script is the best and one of the only props you will ever be able to bring into the audition room. There is no reason the script can't substitute as a magazine, picture, or evidence for all of your "lawyer" scenes and auditions. Remember, in your audition you are required to create the illusion. The only other prop you may bring in is your cell phone, if you are on the phone in your scene. However, please don't forget to turn off your cell phone before walking in the room! Again, your cell phone and script are okay. Otherwise, avoid props at all costs.

Being in the Moment/Letting Go

Most actors don't get the opportunity to audition as often as they would like. So, when you do get called in, it's a great time for you to showcase your talent. Be great. Here's your chance! Show us that you deserve this job. Stay true to the text and stay in the moment. Don't get in your head – you have plenty of time to do that after your audition (which I'm sure you'll do). After all, acting should be fun. Isn't this what you do best? Now show us!

Listening/Taking Direction

Probably the number-one reason actors don't book is because they stop listening. That's number one, so take note! Most of the time, actors are too worried about themselves and what they have to do in the room. You need to take the time to listen to the person you are talking to! If a director, producer, or casting director gives you a note in the audition room, consider this a positive step towards getting called back. It is the director's job to see if you are able to take direction. If you can't take direction in the audition room, you certainly won't be able to on set. Taking direction can be difficult, but is a necessity in becoming a working actor. Here are some helpful hints to stay in the moment:

I know that if a casting director, director, or producer gave me direction in the room, I would want to make sure that I got it right. If you are in a producer session and you don't feel that you can make a quick adjustment, go ahead and ask if you could have a couple of minutes outside the audition room to incorporate the new notes. Remember, just because you are asking for additional time doesn't always mean that you will get it. The casting director probably has 10 or 15 additional actors anxiously waiting to be seen, so it doesn't hurt you to ask for some additional time to get it right. How great would it be if you had some additional time to work on those notes? You might as well ask.

(Note: This is only recommended for producer sessions. If you are in a pre-read with the casting director and the casting director gives you a note, do your best in the room.) If you feel, however, that you can incorporate what they are asking you to do in the room, go for it – just make sure it's right!

Raising the Stakes

It's so important to start thinking about the choices your fellow actors will be bringing in. In other words, it's time to size up your competition and think about what, if anything, gives you an edge. Look around the waiting room and size up your competition. Don't let them, or anything, get in the way of doing your job! Without pushing your scene, think about what your competition will be bringing into their audition—and then top them one notch. From bringing in larger levels, to letting the casting director see your personality before you begin, stand out in the most positive way. Remember: You never hear about the actor who almost books the job, only the one that did.

Show No Hesitation

As an actor, you will need to be able to adapt to many different audition situations, and you should always expect the unexpected. For example, if you plan to sit for your audition and there isn't a chair available for you to sit in, make the adjustment and stand. Don't ask the casting director to get up and get you a chair. Actors should always be able to adapt to the situation that presents itself. If you prefer standing, and the casting director asks you to sit down as you enter the room, make the adjustment. Maybe the casting director wants to talk to you before you begin. You are an actor, commit to your decisions, but please make one. If casting has a preference on whether or not they would like you to sit or stand, they will tell you.

Pace of the Scene

As I have mentioned earlier, it's so important that you allow the audience to catch up to the joke when you are auditioning for a comedy. Continue to breathe through your lines and move your scene forward. This is especially true for any half-hour sitcoms or single-camera comedies. For your dramatic work, continue to move the scene, as the audience will still need to catch up to the action in the scene. You may have beats, or moments within a dramatic scene. Remember, you control the pace of the scene, not the reader. You may even have the time to talk to, or play to multiple characters, if the material warrants it. However, be careful not to get too caught up in your moments, as this can also slow you down in the audition room. Treat the casting director as your audience, who at times will have a very short attention span. If your scene ends up going too slow, you will lose your audience, and not get called back.

Making Strong Choices

It is your job as an actor to make strong choices with the material, which has nothing to do with knowing or memorizing your lines. Let me repeat that: *Making strong choices has nothing to do with knowing your lines.* Knowing your lines is step one. Now, let's bring in steps 2 through 100. Bringing in strong choices has more to do with character development and having a true connection. Take the time to get familiar with the material, so you are connected to the reader, and not the paper. Think about the choices you will need to make as an actor in order to book the job. What will you need to do to connect in the audition room? What risk, good or bad, did you take? Imagine if you were casting this role. Tell me about the actor who booked the job. What did they look like? What did they do with the material to get themselves noticed? Start thinking with the end result in mind.

Dropping Ego Barriers

What does dropping ego barriers mean? To put it simply, don't let "you" get in the way of "you." It's your job as an actor to come in and be professional, not desperate. Leave your ego at the door, let go, and do your job. If the casting director gives you an adjustment with the material, take that as a positive sign—there's interest. Don't take it personally; remember, it's not about you. It's a job, and every CD expects you to do it well.

Mental Training

As an actor, rejection is part of your business. Network executives, studio executives, producers, directors, writers, casting directors, acting coaches, actors, friends, family members, friends of family members, your children, your dog—all of them will or have at one time said, "No." "No" to being an actor. "No" to not being talented enough. "No" to not making enough money. "No" to not making *any* money. "No" because it's too hard. "No." Get used to it. The word "no" lacks any kind of emotional commitment. Yes, it's true: There is a lot of risk to being an actor, but there is also the potential for great success in an industry that discovers new actors on a daily basis. You may and probably will be rejected thousands of times in your career. It's okay.

Being a Local Hire

Being a local hire allows a casting director to hire an actor at a local rate, which is significantly less when it comes down to overall costs. In order to be considered as a local hire, talent must have access to a local address where the project is shooting, or be able to provide a local address of a friend or family member. When I was working on Early Edition with Kyle Chandler, we would cast all of the leading roles in Los Angeles, even though the series was shot in Chicago, Illinois. If I was an actor, I would target the LA casting director to let them know that I was a local hire in Chicago. Hopefully, this will give you another opportunity to audition. The next step is up to you: booking the job. Once that step has been completed (nothing to it, right?), you would then fly yourself to Chicago, put yourself up with family or friends, and do the work. Once you have completed filming, you would then fly yourself back to Los Angeles and continue to audition. Being a local hire can save a production company thousands of dollars, if applicable.

CHAPTER 7

HOW TO HELP YOURSELF

Taking Control Of Your Career

I always tell my actors not to settle. Don't settle with your agency representation. Don't settle with finding that perfect thumbnail or headshot, (It's out there!) Don't settle for the roles you audition for, even if it's just been offered to you. Too many actors settle with what they have. We expect you to excel at your craft. If you're not good at cold reading, take a cold reading class. If you're not good at audition technique, and making strong choices in the audition room, take an audition technique class. If you're not booking commercials, take an improv class. If you don't have a reel, work hard to get one. Don't just settle for not having a reel; you'll need one! In fact, don't settle at all, and see how far you get by expecting more.

Be Your Own Agent

Until you find representation (commercially, theatrically, or otherwise), you will be doing the legwork, acting as your own agent. This includes submitting yourself through some of the online sites we have talked about in this book. For now, go ahead and submit yourself, knowing that you will be limited until you find representation. Managers and agents who are registered with Breakdown Services pay a monthly service fee of $216.00 per month. Remember, the breakdowns let agents and managers know what's being cast on a daily basis, and include SAG, AFTRA,

Equity and non-union projects. Again, this information is only accessible to agents or managers who pay for the service, and is not available to actors.

Actors may continue to submit themselves on Actors Access, Now Casting, and LA Casting until they find representation. Some actors may continue to stay pro-active and submit themselves well after signing with an agent or manager. Eventually, however, you will need to find representation in order to reach your theatrical goals. Do your research and find out who the best agents and managers are and how they are perceived by different casting companies. If you are looking for representation, be open to submitting your material to the agents and managers. There are over 200 SAG-franchised agencies and over 700 managers in Los Angeles alone. It's important for you to know who will be able to move your career forward. Send an 8-by-10 picture along with a resume and small cover letter, letting them know exactly what you are looking for. You'll see fairly quickly what kind of interest your headshots are generating. Remember, it's okay to submit for representation on a somewhat regular basis—every six months or until you have received a response. It's always best to look for representation during the slower months – November, December, May and June. Once pilot season begins, agents and managers slow down their search for new talent. It's hard enough for agents and managers to get auditions for their current roster of clients, let alone new clients.

Write Yourself Something

If you are having trouble putting together a demo reel, it may be time for you to start writing your own material. Agents, managers, and casting directors are always going to ask to see what you look like on film, especially when you are being considered for theatrical representation. Write an ensemble piece, with three to four pages of dialogue, starring you. Borrow a digital video camera and start shooting! There are companies that can do this for you, but try to do this on your own first, to save money. Your main expense will be to hire a professional editor. You will need a reel, so don't settle for not having one. As long as it looks like an independent film and makes you look good, it's probably usable.

SAG Rates: Money to Be Made

There is money to be made being a SAG actor. Currently, the minimum amount of money a SAG actor can make for one day is $809.00. This is known as SAG scale. You may, however, get booked for two, three, five or eight days, which would increase your overall rate. As you work more, your day rate, or the amount of money you make per day will increase. The goal is to always try and increase your daily rate, or quote. Casting directors are supposed to honor an actor's day quote, so actors are never paid less than what they made on their previous job. However, a CD will always try and negotiate a lower pricing point during negotiations, to save the production company money. Even though this tug-of-war exists, agents should always ask for more money for his or her client. This doesn't mean that the actor will always get more, but the agent should at least ask. If you end up making less than your last job, your agent may request a "no quote," which blocks other CD's from obtaining specific deal points, including what you were paid. A "no quote" is useful when an actor has agreed to work for less than their original quote, and doesn't want this information shared.

Surround Yourself with Working Actors

Some acting classes in Los Angeles may cost you as much as your rent. Try to find a class that will allow you to perform with actors who are working. Audit as many classes as you can. You don't necessarily have to spend a lot to get a lot. Find a class that will push you and get you out of your comfort zone. You don't need to be the best actor in the class. You do, however, need to find a teacher that will motivate you, so you can reach your full potential. I don't know any actors who are comfortable in the audition room, so why should class be any different?

Enjoy the Process

It is now time for you to create your business plan. Go back to the beginning and start to develop a plan for your new business—the business of YOU. Develop each step until it has been completed, and keep focused on what you have to do in order for your business to grow. It won't be easy, but nothing good ever is.

"All your life you are told the things you cannot do. All your life they will say you're not good enough or strong enough or talented enough; They will say you're the wrong height or the wrong weight or the wrong type to play this or be this or achieve this. They will tell you no, a thousand times no, until all the no's become meaningless. All your life they will tell you no, quite firmly and very quickly. They will tell you no. And you will tell them **YES.**"

Nike